Prayi..g

for Unsaved Loved Ones

SERVE

Praying
for Unsaved Loved Ones

A simple and effective model for New Testament intercession

Billy & Kirsty Lummis

Published in 2015 by Serve, an imprint of Great Big Life Publishing
Empower Centre, 83-87 Kingston Road, Portsmouth, PO2 7DX, UK

British Library Cataloguing in Publication Data.

A catalogue record for this book is available from the British Library.

Scriptures from the King James Version unless otherwise stated, and all underlined emphasis by author.

CONTENTS

FOREWORD FROM THE AUTHORS

As teachers to the body of Christ we believe, as Paul charged Timothy, that we are called to preach the Word. The Bible says that God has magnified His Word above all His name (Psalm 138:2) and that God's Word is forever settled in heaven (Psalm 119:89). His Word is perfect and restores the whole person (Psalm 19:7); His Word heals and delivers us (Psalm 107:20); His Word is alive and powerful, sharper than any two-edged sword (Hebrews 4:12); His words are spirit and life (John 6:63)! God's Word is our ultimate rule for faith and action.

An anointed teacher will take what is complicated and make it simple. An annoying teacher will take what is simple and make it complicated!

This book therefore is short and simple by design. We have found that the more simply we receive the Word of God the more likely we are to do it – and that is the important thing. As it says in the book of James, we are to become 'doers of the word and not hearers only, deceiving our own selves' (James 1:22).

In writing this book we hope to provide a simple and effective model for New Testament intercessory prayer, that believers will find the time in their everyday life to take and do! We hope also that this in turn will see thousands come to the saving knowledge of Jesus and that He would be glorified!

As for a dedication of this book: all for Jesus, the Altogether Lovely One!

His,
Billy and Kirsty

INTRODUCTION

In this book we will be looking at how to make New Testament intercession for an unsaved person by using a simple and effective model of prayer based on the scriptures.

Intercession is simply prayer made on behalf of another person. It is unlikely that our unsaved loved ones will be praying for their own salvation, but we certainly can! An example of a New Testament intercessor is Epaphras, who prayed for people in Colosse.

> *Epaphras, who is one of you, a servant of Christ, saluteth you, always labouring fervently for you in prayers, that ye may stand perfect and complete in all the will of God.*
>
> ***(Colossians 4:12)***

A spiritual battle is taking place for the soul

of every person, as Jesus seeks to save the lost, and satan tries to deceive and draw mankind away from God.

All believers are part of this battle. If you are born again, God has called, equipped, and empowered you through His Spirit to minister and touch other people's lives. And one of our first ministries is to pray.

> *I exhort therefore, that, first of all, supplications, prayers, intercessions, and giving of thanks be made for all men.*
>
> ***(1 Timothy 2:1)***

God strongly encourages us to pray for ALL people – not just the ones we like, but ALL!

Every believer is called to this responsibility and ministry.

I'm sure most would agree that God would never ask His people to do something that was a waste of their time, or void of any effect. God has a purpose for everything He says or does. If our prayers had no influence, or perhaps had only influence in the lives of some people, then why would God instruct us to pray for ALL? So we can see that, as the Holy Spirit encourages us through Paul to pray for ALL men, this must mean that there is not one person who is outside the scope of being touched by God through the prayers of believers. Every single man, woman and child on this earth is able to be influenced and moved by the Spirit of God IF WE PRAY and WHEN WE PRAY!

Although we understand that God will not violate the will of an individual and force them to get saved, as Ephesians 2:8 states that "for by grace are ye saved through faith". Therefore it is still an individual's responsibility and choice of their will to put faith in the salvation that God has provided by grace and so receive it into their lives. However, our prayers can still carry great effectiveness and power in the spiritual realm and, in the battle for every individual soul to receive Jesus, I have no doubt that countless people have been brought to salvation through the influence of praying believers.

James 5:16 states that "the effectual fervent prayer of a righteous man availeth much."

1

EFFECTIVE PRAYER AND GOD'S WILL

Now before we start I just want to say that prayer is a very individual thing that differs from person to person, and whilst we will be looking at ways that we can all pray effectively, it is not to say that you have to pray this way, or that if you don't pray this way then you're wrong. However, we can make our prayers more effective towards saving the lost when we find out how to pray in accordance with God's Word and His will.

> *For the word of God is quick, and powerful,*
> *and sharper than any two-edged sword,*

> *piercing even to the dividing asunder of soul and spirit, and of the joints and marrow, and is a discerner of the thoughts and intents of the heart.*
>
> ***(Hebrews 4:12)***

The Bible shows us that God and His Word are one and that God's Word is His will:

> *In the beginning was the Word, and the Word was with God, and the Word was God.*
>
> ***(John 1:1)***

God and His Word are one and that is why God will never violate His Word:

> *God is not a man, that he should lie; neither the son of man, that he should repent: hath he said, and shall he not do it? or hath he spoken, and shall he not make it good?*
>
> ***(Numbers 23:19)***

My covenant will I not break, nor alter the thing that is gone out of my lips.

(Psalm 89:34)

You cannot operate outside the Word of God and be in the will of God. So when we pray God's Word we are praying His will. Now look at what the scripture says about praying according to God's will.

And this is the confidence that we have in him, that, if we ask any thing according to his will, he heareth us: And if we know that he hear us, whatsoever we ask, we know that we have the petitions that we desired of him.

(1 John 5:14-15)

To pray God's Word is to pray God's will, and when we pray God's will we have confidence that God has heard and that we have received what we have prayed for. So, for our prayers to be heard and to be effective, we want to be praying in accordance with God's Word. Praying in faith according to God's Word releases power and gets answers!

2

GOD WANTS THEM SAVED!

When it comes to praying effectively the motivation of our heart is very important. Paul said in 1 Corinthians 13:3:

> *And though I bestow all my goods to feed the poor, and though I give my body to be burned, and have not charity, it profiteth me nothing.*

Paul could give away everything he owned and even sacrifice his own life for others, but he says, "If I don't do it out of a heart motivation of love, it will profit me nothing!"

In James 4 the scripture shows us that

people were praying and asking God for things, but because their heart motivation was not right (it was based on their wrong lustful and selfish desires), they did not receive what they were asking for.

> *Ye ask, and receive not, because ye ask amiss, that ye may consume it upon your lusts.*
>
> ***(James 4:3)***

With God, our heart attitude is just as important as what we are saying, and many approach God when making intercession for the lost with a wrong attitude.

They may come to God in prayer believing that God is up there in heaven angry with the world, withholding mercy, and that they have to beg and plead with God to get Him to move and save their loved ones.

Some of those things may have been true in the Old Testament, because of people's sin and rebellion against God, but we are now under the New Testament and that makes a difference in how we should approach God when making intercession for the unsaved. We want to come to God with the right heart motivation and attitude.

One of the first things to recognise when praying for the lost to receive salvation is that God is on our side, or rather, we are on His side. We never have to try to move God and make Him save someone. Salvation was His idea! God wants the lost saved infinitely more than we do. God is not withholding salvation from anyone.

God's desire is that no-one should perish but that all come to receive the wonderful gift of salvation that He has provided through Jesus.

Ezekiel 33:11 (NKJV) says, "Say to them: 'As I live,' says the Lord God, 'I have no pleasure in the death of the wicked, but that the wicked turn from his way and live.'"

Peter tells us in the New Testament,

> *"The Lord is not slack concerning His promise, as some count slackness, but is*

longsuffering toward us, not willing that any should perish but that all should come to repentance."

(2 Peter 3:9, NKJV)

1 Timothy 2:4 states that God ". . . will have all men to be saved, and to come unto the knowledge of the truth."

So it is God's will that all people should be saved. Through Jesus' death, burial and resurrection, the price has been paid for the whole world to be able to receive salvation through faith in His Son Jesus Christ.

For God so loved the world, that he gave his only begotten Son, that whosoever believeth in him should not perish, but have everlasting life.

(John 3:16)

For whosoever shall call upon the name of the Lord shall be saved.

(Romans 10:13)

'Whosoever' covers every person! Is your unsaved loved one a 'whosoever'? Then they qualify for God's grace!

We don't have to plead with God in prayer to pour out His mercy towards the lost or to turn from His wrath and judgement – He has already extended all mercy to them through Jesus Christ and in this period of time God is extending grace to all people.

> *For the grace of God that bringeth salvation hath appeared to all men.*
>
> ***(Titus 2:11)***

God is not angry towards people, He's not even in a bad mood!

> *Glory to God in the highest, and on earth peace, good will toward men.*
>
> ***(Luke 2:14)***

Notice, not peace among men, but peace toward men, from God. God is not holding their sins against them.

> *For God was in Christ, reconciling the world to himself, no longer counting people's sins against them. And he gave us this wonderful message of reconciliation.*
> ***(2 Corinthians 5:19, NLT)***

In the Old Testament God did hold men's sins against them as we can read about in many cases, but now under the new covenant things are different.

It is not that God is unjust or has turned a blind eye to sin, but that two thousand years ago, at the cross of Calvary, God poured out His wrath and judgement for the sins of the world in the body of His Son, Jesus Christ.

> *He [Jesus Christ] himself is the sacrifice that atones for our sins-and not only our sins but the sins of all the world.*
> ***(1 John 2:2, NLT)***

From the previous scriptures we can see that salvation is God's will for every person and that Jesus has already paid the full price so that every lost person can receive salvation freely today.

> *Behold, now [is] the accepted time;*
> *behold, now [is] the day of salvation.*
>
> ***(2 Corinthians 6:2)***

The problem therefore lies, not with God being angry or withholding mercy from any lost person, but that the lost are not believing and receiving what God has already done for them.

The Bible shows that salvation is by grace alone through faith alone in Christ alone. (see Ephesians 2:8-9, John 14:6, Acts 4:12).

If you are reading this book and you have personally never received Jesus into your heart and you wish to do so, please turn to the Salvation Prayer at the back of the book which you can pray and immediately receive Jesus as your Saviour.

Now our motivation and efforts in prayer as New Testament intercessors is simply to work with God's Spirit to help the lost receive the salvation that has already been provided for them freely by His grace.

God wants to reach out and touch all of unsaved humanity, (that includes our unsaved friends and relatives) and God needs to flow through His body on the earth today – that is, every born again believer, for we are the body of Christ. God is going to use our prayers, our faith, and our words to release His power and Spirit towards the lost to show them His love and grace and to convict them of their need for Him.

3

SO HOW CAN WE START?

Let's look at how God's Word says we can make New Testament intercession for the unsaved.

Remember the most effective way that we can pray is when we pray according to the Word and will of God. (see Hebrews 4:12, John 5:14-15)

We can start with thanksgiving. Psalm 100:4 says, "enter into His gates with thanksgiving and into His courts with praise, be thankful unto Him and bless His name."

We don't want to be coming before God and saying, "Oh God, where are you? It's been twenty years and Uncle John still isn't saved

– he's worse than he ever was, I don't know what to do, it looks like he'll never get saved, it looks like there's no hope."

All that kind of prayer will do is minister doubt, unbelief and discouragement to yourself. God knows about the whole situation even before we start to pray. Instead we can begin our prayer with thanksgiving and praise.

> *"Thank You, Father, that You love Uncle John so much that while he was still a sinner you gave your only Son to die for him. Thank You that You've already made the provision for his salvation. Thank You, Father, that it's Your will and desire that he be saved and come to know Jesus."*

Praying like that not only glorifies God, but it will also minister faith to you and enables you to encourage yourself in the Lord.

So we are now coming before God in faith, but we know that the problem is simply that our loved ones are not receiving the salvation that God has already provided, and desires for them to experience.

4

WHY DON'T THEY BELIEVE IN JESUS?

Next, as New Testament intercessors we can begin to pray effectively to influence and bring change in that lost person's life, and to bring them to faith in Jesus.

Now we need to recognise and identify what is stopping the lost person from seeing and receiving the truth of the Gospel. The Bible shows us:

> *But if our gospel be hid, it is hid to them that are lost: In whom the god of this world hath blinded the minds of them which believe not, lest the light of the*

glorious gospel of Christ, who is the image of God, should shine unto them.

(2 Corinthians 4:3-4)

This scripture says, "to them that are lost: In whom . . ." Notice the scripture doesn't say "to some that are lost: In some . . ." This scripture is talking about ALL that are lost. This scripture says that the reason why any lost person is not receiving the Gospel of Christ is because the good news is being hidden from them. Their minds are being blinded by demonic deception (satan, referred to above as 'the god of this world'), which is hindering them from seeing the truth of the Gospel.

This does not mean that they are possessed, or evil people, but simply that their minds have been deceived in some way by the demonic influences that are at work in this world. These can be thoughts, philosophies, concepts, or wisdom, which are contrary to the Word of God; it may be negative experiences or past hurts.

They may think that people only invite them to church because the church wants their money. Maybe they believe that there is no God; that we just evolved, or perhaps dry "religion" has hardened their hearts to God.

When we have witnessed to people, often they will say that they don't believe for these kinds of reasons.

A common belief that we have experienced is that people think that if you are simply a 'good person' then God will accept you, not realizing that it is only by faith in Christ that saves them, not their performance (Ephesians 2:8-9). Others think that the lives they have lived makes them too bad for God to be able to receive them, so never reach out in faith because they believe they have disqualified themselves.

It is just as often the case that people have either never heard, or never understood the true gospel message of God's grace and so therefore have not been able to receive salvation.

Whatever reasons they have, they are simply

believing the demonic lies of the enemy and being blinded in their minds – like placing a veil over their eyes, hiding the truth of the gospel of God's love and grace which prevents them from receiving salvation.

So, although a lost person has a free will to make choices for themselves, their decision not to receive Christ is actually being influenced by satan, who is blinding their minds and causing them to believe a deception that is hindering them from receiving the truth of the gospel of Jesus Christ.

This is an important truth to realise because although we cannot pray to change the will of another human being, through the prayer of intercession we can come against and bind the demonic forces that are influencing their choices and blinding their minds and hearts.

The apostle Paul said that Jesus told him to go into a lost world, "to open their eyes, and to turn them from darkness to light, and from the power of satan unto God, that they may receive forgiveness of sins, and inheritance among them which are sanctified by faith that is in me," (Acts 26:18). A major part of Paul's ministry was to destroy demonic deceptions that blinded people to the truth.

Now we as New Testament believers can take authority over wrong influences so that our loved ones can make a truly 'free willed' decision about the Gospel, and we can do this because every New Testament believer has been given authority by God, through faith in the Name of Jesus, over all the power and works of the devil.

Jesus said in Luke 10:19 "Behold I give unto you power, (Greek: authority) to tread on serpents and scorpions (demonic forces), and over all the power (Greek: ability) of the enemy and nothing shall by any means hurt you." *(brackets mine)*

And these signs shall follow them that believe;
In my name shall they cast out devils.

(Mark 16:17)

If you only have authority over the enemies' activities in your own life then you don't really have authority over all his works, which is what Jesus stated. You would just have a limited authority over your own life. But Jesus said we have authority over all the works of the enemy, wherever they may be.

Likewise, in Matthew 18:18 Jesus tells us that we can bind and loose things in prayer: "Verily I say unto you, Whatsoever ye shall bind on earth shall be bound in heaven: and whatsoever ye shall loose on earth shall be loosed in heaven."

Notice that we are the ones told to do the binding and loosing first on earth! It begins with us!

We are also told in the Word of God to resist and cast out the devil's influence from our lives and the lives of others.

> *Submit yourselves therefore to God. Resist the devil, and he will flee from you.*
>
> ***(James 4:7)***

This scripture does not say "ask God to resist the devil for you." It says YOU resist the devil and he will flee from YOU! Not from God, but from you. Now it's God's power in us, but we are the ones who have been given the authority and responsibility to release that power and resist. Therefore, through prayer, we can take authority over the devil's influence on our unsaved loved ones. Our authority comes through faith in the name of Jesus.

Philippians 2:10 says that, at the name of Jesus, every knee should bow, of things in heaven, and things in earth, and things under the earth. Therefore we can take authority in our loved ones lives; not over their will, but over the negative forces trying to influence them. For example, if you are praying for your child, you can pray: "satan, I command you in the name of Jesus to take your hands off my child. I bind every evil influence that is blinding their mind to the truth of the Gospel, I break your hold on them and command your activities against them to cease. Loose them now in Jesus' name."

The great thing with praying in the spiritual realm is that it is not limited to distance or space. You can pray for the lost wherever they are in the world. Your love can still touch someone on the other side of the world, and likewise so can your faith.

We can see an example of someone who was not limited by distance when the Syrophoenician woman came to Jesus (Mark chapter 7); it was on behalf of her daughter who had a devil. Through the mother's faith, her daughter was delivered even though she wasn't physically present with Jesus or her mother.

Now I believe that there are spiritual principals that determine the level of influence that your prayers have over another person. For example, I believe you have greater authority over the influences in your own house and children than an outsider would have. This is true both in the natural and the spiritual realm. You also have more impact when praying for someone if that person is under, or yielding to your authority.

However, although every Christian has been given authority over the devil, we do not have ultimate authority in another human's life, so although we pray like this it does not remove all wrong thinking and wrong doing from that person's life. But through our authority in Jesus' name we can hinder and resist the demonic influences that are trying to stop them from receiving salvation.

So you see that praying for the lost is not a one-time prayer. Although we have ultimate authority for the choices in our own lives, when we're praying for another person, especially if they may not even be wanting us to pray for them, they have the right, (or the authority) to choose what they are influenced by. So even though we can disrupt the enemy's influence in their lives, their deception could be so deeply rooted that they can, despite our prayers, choose deception again. Therefore we do not pray these prayers just once, but continue in our intercession for them until we see change.

Continue in prayer, and watch in the same with thanksgiving.

(Colossians 4:2)

Remember we read in 1 Timothy 2:1: "I exhort therefore, that, first of all, supplications, prayers, intercessions, and giving of thanks, be made for all men."

Notice that the words "supplications, prayers, intercessions, and giving of thanks" all have something in common: they all end with an 's'. That means you're going to need to do them more than once! We should develop a lifestyle of prayer but it should never become a heavy burden for us. Jesus, who came to seek and save the lost, said, "For my yoke is easy and my burden is light" (Matthew 11:30).

So the next way in which we can pray for our lost loved ones according to the Word, is to consistently bind the wrong influences that are blinding them from receiving the truth of the Gospel.

5

THEY NEED TO HEAR

It obviously is not enough to just come against wrong influences. For a person to be saved they must also receive the right influence. The Word of God says in Ephesians 2:8, "For by grace are ye saved through faith; and that not of yourselves: it is the gift of God."

This faith needed for salvation comes from hearing the Word of God.

> *So then faith cometh by hearing, and hearing by the word of God.*
>
> ***(Romans 10:17)***

> *For whosoever shall call upon the name of*

the Lord shall be saved. How then shall they call on him in whom they have not believed? and how shall they believe in him of whom they have not heard? and how shall they hear without a preacher?

(Romans 10:13-14)

These scriptures show that for our unsaved loved ones to be born again they must also hear the truth of God's Word.

Being born again, not of corruptible seed, but of incorruptible, by the word of God, which liveth and abideth for ever.

(1 Peter 1:23)

Every single person receives salvation through the Word of God in some way. So before a lost person can ever be born again, they have to hear the Word. The lost have to have circumstances in their life through which the Word of God can be planted and sown into their hearts.

This is another area where the Bible tells us that we can pray and intercede for our loved ones, because our prayers can affect circumstances and help to create situations that would bring them into contact with the Lord Jesus through His Word. God knows who our unsaved loved ones will listen to. He knows how to bring those people or influences into their lives at just the right time.

Jesus Himself invites us to pray and intercede like this for the lost:

> *Pray ye therefore the Lord of the harvest, that he will send forth labourers into his harvest.*
>
> ***(Matthew 9:38)***

Jesus instructs us as His disciples to pray to God that He will send forth labourers into His harvest. The harvest is all the unsaved people in the World and the labourer is sent to bring the gospel, or you could say, to bring the Word of God regarding salvation to the world.

And he [Jesus] said unto them, Go ye into all the world, and preach the gospel to every creature.

(Mark 16:15)

The sower soweth the word.

(Mark 4:14)

The Word can be sown through many different forms and mediums. It can be preached in person, it can be through media, television, radio, books, tracts, songs, or films. For a person to be born again God sends out His Word and His love into the harvest (the lost) through labourers. So, for example, we can pray:

"Father, I lift up (name of unsaved loved one) to You and I am asking You and speaking out my faith to release Your power right now to send labourers across their path, to sow Your love and Your Word into their life. I pray that today they will tune into and hear Christian

television or radio, even if it's by accident, or pick up and read a magazine with a Christian article. I pray that a believer will come across their path today in love and witness to them. Father, where they work, let one of their clients be a Christian that will speak about Jesus. Father, I pray that you would send Christian school friends into their life that will speak the Word to them."

My Dad came to the Lord late in his life. I had spent time with him talking about Jesus but although he was open-minded, he hadn't seemed to have taken the final step to believe in Jesus and receive salvation. But my Dad loved listening to the radio, and I was delighted one day when he told me that he had listened to a brief programme explaining salvation, and prayed to receive his salvation. I truly believe this 'labourer' was the final thing that led him to believe, and although he has passed on, he is now joyfully with the Lord for eternity.

Sometimes an unsaved relative may respond better to non-family than to their family members.

Another member of my family finally accepted Jesus as their Lord and Saviour, after someone whom they didn't know in church came up to them and said, "So, when did you get born again?". This was a question they couldn't answer, but opened the way for me to explain to them what it meant to be born again, and later that day they gave their heart to the Lord and received their salvation.

Jesus tells us to pray for God to send labourers into the harvest. And He doesn't invite us to pray that way so that He can ignore our prayers. He answers our prayers when we pray, but again, we must realise that it does not guarantee that the person will be saved the next day. There are so many factors that come into play such as the unsaved person's will, how willing they are to receive the Word, and how obedient Christians are to the leading of God's Spirit to actually go and preach the Word.

Jesus has chosen to flow through His body

(believers), so He has to have people who will respond to His leading and go and share God's love and speak the Word. In Acts 9:10-18 we see how God answers prayer by sending a labourer. Verse 11 starts with God saying to Ananias (a believer), "Arise and go." He was a labourer being sent. The verse ends with "for, behold, he (Paul) prays."

We see that at first Ananias seems a little reluctant to go to this notorious man who had been persecuting Christians, and Ananias could have refused God's call. If he had, it would not have been God's lack of answer to Paul's prayer, but the disobedience of God's labourer which would have caused Ananias not to go. However, we see that Ananias was obedient and went to Paul.

Also, as well as the labourer's obedience, we need to consider our loved one's response to them. God may send a believer to go and witness to our relative. The person who God sends may go up to our loved one and say – "I'd like to tell you about Jesus" but our relative might at first say, “No, thanks“ and walk off. Your prayer was answered, but your loved one didn‘t receive.

Paul himself asked the Colossian church to pray for opportunities for him to minister the Word into people’s lives:

> *Continue earnestly in prayer, being vigilant in it with thanksgiving; meanwhile praying also for us, that God would open to us a door for the word, to speak the mystery of Christ.*
>
> **(Colossians 4:2-3, NKJV)**

Being earnest in prayer means to be diligent and continuous until you see the desired result. The person you are interceding for may have resisted the labourer, or may have had the Word sown into their life, but it may take time before you see the fruit of it, so we continue in prayer for the Word again to be sent across their path.

We have a friend who is now loving and

serving God. She told us how that before she came to Jesus and her salvation she would get quite annoyed with the number of people in her life, and even random strangers, who would approach her and say they'd like to talk to her about Jesus or invite her to church. She had a praying Mum! Now her Mum's prayers for labourers to bring the Word to her daughter were being answered, and labourers were being sent, but it took some time before she was ready to receive. But praise God! Her Mum continued earnestly in prayers until her daughter came to salvation.

Now, because a person needs to receive the Word of God before they can be born again, another thing that we can do is to ask the Holy Spirit to bring God's Word back to their remembrance.

Jesus says in John 14:26, "But the Comforter, which is the Holy Ghost, whom the Father will send in my name, he shall teach you all things, and bring all things to your remembrance, whatsoever I have said unto you."

Now Jesus is speaking to His disciples here, but I believe the Holy Spirit does this with every person.

Jesus said in John 6:44 "No man can come to me, except the Father which hath sent me draw him: and I will raise him up at the last day." The Word also states in John 16:8-9 that the Holy Spirit convicts the world of the sin of not believing on Jesus.

Our Father God, through His Holy Spirit, is always seeking to draw lost people to Jesus. The Holy Spirit testifies of Jesus to people and witnesses to their heart, convicting them of their need for a Saviour.

So we can pray and ask the Holy Spirit to bring to our unsaved loved one's remembrance any scriptures that they may have ever heard or read, maybe even just lines on a Christmas card. Perhaps, if they are backslidden, you can pray that the Holy Spirit would bring to their remembrance the things they once knew, to convict them that they need to get right with God.

In Ian McCormack's testimony – a man who was stung by deadly jelly fish during a night dive and, while near death, experienced hell and heaven – he says that, whilst he could feel his body dying, the Holy Spirit had moved on his mother, in another part of the world, to pray for her son. As she did, Her words and the Lord's prayer and scriptures, such as, "God is light and in Him is no darkness at all," (1 John 1:5) which Ian had previously read on a Christmas card, were brought back to his remembrance even after years of being away from God. These things were strong influences in his deathbed repentance, where he gave his life to Jesus. The reason why we know of this salvation is because Jesus restored him to life. His testimony is a very powerful one, but it began with words that had previously been sown in his life.[1]

Another point here is that sometimes we do not need to pray for others to speak the

---

1. For more of Ian McCormack's testimony, visit http://www.aglimpseofeternity.org

Word to our relatives if we could do it. Although it is true that our relatives may respond better to non-family members, we can pray for God to give us the opportunities and the boldness to preach the Word to our families and friends just like the early church did in Acts 4:29 (NLT): "And now, O Lord, hear their threats, and give us, your servants, great boldness in preaching your word."

6

UNDERSTANDING THE WORD

Now, when a lost person hears the Word of God they also have to understand and receive that Word into their heart for it to have an effect.

> *When any one heareth the word of the kingdom, and understandeth [it] not, then cometh the wicked [one], and catcheth away that which was sown in his heart. This is he which received seed by the way side.*
>
> ***(Matthew 13:19)***

A lost person needs to understand the Word

of God and the message of salvation for it to take root in their heart, so another scriptural prayer that we can pray for our unsaved loved ones is found in the first chapter of the book of Ephesians. Paul prays:

> *That the God of our Lord Jesus Christ, the Father of glory, may give unto you the spirit of wisdom and revelation in the knowledge of him: The eyes of your understanding being enlightened; that ye may know what is the hope of his calling, and what the riches of the glory of his inheritance in the saints.*
>
> ***(Ephesians 1:17-18)***

We can pray that God would give our loved ones the spirit of wisdom and revelation in the knowledge of Jesus so that the eyes of their understanding (their heart) might be enlightened, giving them the understanding of God's grace and the revelation of who Jesus really is, and their need for a Saviour.

As we read earlier in Acts chapter 26, the apostle Paul said that Jesus told him to go into a lost world:

> *To open their eyes, and to turn them from darkness to light, and from the power of Satan unto God, that they may receive forgiveness of sins, and inheritance among them which are sanctified by faith that is in me.*
>
> ***(Acts 26:18)***

Notice that first of all, a lost person's eyes, or you could say their heart or understanding, has to be opened before they are turned from darkness to light. So we can also pray that they might see and come to know God's love and goodness towards them, because the Word says that it is "the goodness of God that leadeth thee to repentance." (Romans 2:4)

In our Bible study group we recently prayed with the grandparents of a teenager who they were taking on a Christian youth camp, that his eyes would be opened and his heart softened so that he could receive the salvation messages he would hear. And praise God, he returned from that camp confessing that he had been born again!

7

BELIEVE THAT YOU RECEIVE THE ANSWER TO YOUR PRAYERS

We have highlighted three main areas where we can make effective intercession on behalf of an unsaved loved one according to the Word and will of God. The Bible says that we should believe that we receive these things when we pray.

> *And all things, whatsoever ye shall ask in prayer, believing, ye shall receive.*
>
> ***(Matthew 21:22)***

In the book of James it tells us that we should pray and ask in faith, not wavering in doubt or unbelief. "But let him ask in faith, nothing wavering" (James 1:6). So knowing that God wants our loved ones to come to salvation, and the things in His Word on how to effectively pray, we can finish our prayers with thanksgiving knowing that God has answered our prayers. It is good to thank God for answering our prayers and also for everything that He is doing, seen and unseen, in the lives of those we are praying for.

A SIMPLE PRAYER OUTLINE

We begin and end our prayer with thanksgiving for all that God has done and is doing, (Psalm 100:4) and we have three points in between:

- We take authority over and bind the wrong influences that are blinding the mind of that person from receiving the Gospel.
  (2 Corinthians 4:4)

- We pray for labourers to bring God's Word across their path. (Matthew 9:38, 1 Peter 1:23 and John 14:26)
- We pray for the spirit of wisdom and revelation to be released through God's Spirit and Word. (Ephesians 1:17-18)

Again, you don't have to pray like this, and you're not wrong if you don't, so just take from these points whatever you feel may help you.

How diligent you want to be with your prayers is up to you. You might want to pray once a day, you might want to pray once a week, that's really up to you, as you feel led or as is appropriate in your situation.

You can also use this model of prayer for yourself or for anyone even if they are already saved.

For example you may have children who are saved, but you can still use this model to intercede for them to walk out their destiny according to the will of God.

You can:

- Thank God for them, and that they are saved
- Take authority over any evil that may be trying to influence and affect their lives.
- Pray for labourers to come across their path in the form of godly role models, friends and influences, such as music, etc.
- Pray for God to give them the wisdom and revelation in the knowledge of Him so that they will come to know Jesus in a greater way and walk in all His provision and destiny for their life.

Really, you can use and adapt this model of prayer when you pray for anyone, whether it be family, church leaders, or Governmental leaders.

This is just a really simple and effective model prayer that you can pray, and have confidence in your prayers because you know that you are praying in accordance with God's Word and His will.

Although prayer alone cannot guarantee that your loved ones will be saved (because ultimately that is their choice), you can guarantee that it will bring them under conviction and that it will affect and influence the circumstances in their lives as you make effective intercession for them.

And be expectant that you will have the joy of seeing them come to the saving knowledge of Jesus Christ!

EXAMPLE SALVATION PRAYER FOR A LOVED ONE

> *"Father, thank you that it is Your will that all should come to the saving knowledge of Jesus Christ, and this includes [insert name]. I take my authority in Christ and I command everything that is blinding them to the truth of the gospel, and that is hindering them from receiving the truth to GO from them now in the Name of Jesus. I ask that you*

would send labourers into (name's) life that would bring the Word across their path, and that the eyes of their understanding will be enlightened so that they can see and receive the truth of the gospel and Your goodness, which leads them to repentance. Father thank You for all that you are doing in their lives, thank You for their salvation, in the Name of Jesus."

(Based on: 2 Peter 3:9, Matthew 9:38, Ephesians 1:18, Romans 2:4, Luke 10:19)

Now don't give up! Even if things don't seem to change, keep praying over them, and confessing the promises of God over their life. Thank God for all He is doing in their life. And God's Spirit, through your faith filled prayers, is causing things to happen!

Devote yourselves to prayer with an alert mind and a thankful heart.

(Colossians 4:2, NLT)

8

CLOSING THOUGHTS

In this book we have used a simple model according to the will and Word of God with three main areas that we can pray with our understanding so that it is easy to remember and not too time consuming to do.

However, there are also other effective things that we can do when interceding for the lost which we have not gone into but wanted to mention, such as:

PRAYING IN TONGUES

If you are able, you can pray in tongues and let the Holy Spirit make intercession through you that way. The Holy Spirit knows what needs to be prayed and done in every situation, far more than we do with our limited understanding. When we pray in tongues we allow the Holy Spirit to pray into the situations through us. (Romans 8:26-27).

THE PRAYER OF AGREEMENT

You can also pray effectively with a prayer partner, joining with another believer in the prayer of agreement. Jesus said, "I also tell you this: If two of you agree here on earth concerning anything you ask, my Father in heaven will do it for you. For where two or three gather together as my followers, I am there among them."(Matthew 18:19-20, NLT)

Praying with another believer can also encourage you, and you can pray for each other's loved ones too.

SPEAKING POSITIVE WORDS OF FAITH.

The Bible also says in Proverbs 18:21, "Death and life are in the power of the tongue: and they that love it shall eat the fruit thereof." So we can release life over our unsaved loved ones lives by speaking good things about them.

The Bible tells is to "Therefore be imitators of God as dear children. (Ephesians 5:1, NKJV), and also says that:

> *God, who quickeneth the dead, and calleth those things which be not as though they were.*
>
> ***(Romans 4:17)***

God speaks blessing, peace and righteousness over His children, even when our daily walk may not look exactly like this, as we have not yet received by faith the fullness of all such blessings. So, whatever the situation and circumstances might look like in a lost person's life, we can imitate God our Father and call those things which be "not as though they were." We can declare over their lives things like: "My husband is a mighty man of God", "All of my family belongs to Jesus," and, "As for me and my house, we will serve the Lord" (Joshua 24:15). We can speak Spirit-filled words of life and faith into the situation to bring about change.

Even though circumstances may look the same and our loved ones seem the same after we have been praying, in faith we can declare over them and call them saved, loving God and walking in God's destiny for their lives.

LIVE LIVES THAT ADORN THE GOSPEL!

As well as praying for our unsaved loved ones, we can also influence them by our lives and the way in which we represent our own faith, making salvation something to be desired.

Peter advises believers to live godly lives, saying,

> *Be careful to live properly among your unbelieving neighbours. Then even if they accuse you of doing wrong, they will see your honourable behaviour, and they will give honor to God when he judges the world.*
>
> ***(1 Peter 2:12, NLT)***

Peter also encourages believing women to have godly lives for their unsaved husbands' sake:

> *In the same way, you wives must accept the authority of your husbands. Then, even if some refuse to obey the Good News, your godly lives will speak to them without any words. They will be won over by observing your pure and reverent lives.*
>
> ***(1 Peter 3:1-2, NLT)***

The world is quick to judge believers and can be turned off from God by believers who are unkind, judgemental, or who act in a hypocritical way saying one thing and acting in another way. But when our lives reflect the goodness of God we can adorn the gospel; that is to make the message of the gospel attractive to the lost.

Paul tells Titus to exhort believing slaves:

> *Slaves must always obey their masters and*

> *do their best to please them. They must not talk back or steal, but must show themselves to be entirely trustworthy and good. Then they will make the teaching about God our Saviour attractive in every way.*
>
> ***(Titus 2:9 NLT)***

Our behaviour does not replace the need for the lost in our families or workplaces to hear the Word of God, but it is an important factor because it strongly influences them when it comes to receiving God's salvation.

Do you know Jesus personally?

PRAYER FOR SALVATION AND THE HOLY SPIRIT

Knowing Jesus and making Him the Lord of your life is the greatest thing anyone can do.

If you would like to know Jesus for yourself, this relationship begins with inviting Jesus into your heart.

The Bible says that:

> *If you confess with your mouth the Lord Jesus and believe in your heart that God has raised Him from the dead, you will be saved. For with the heart one believed unto righteousness, and with the mouth confession is made unto salvation.*
>
> ***(Romans 10:9-10)***

> *For whosoever shall call upon the name of the Lord shall be saved.*
>
> ***(Romans 10:13)***

When you confess Jesus as your Lord, believing in your heart that God raised Him from the dead, you are born again, which means that you receive forgiveness of sins, and are made right with God. You receive a new life from God and become a brand new person on the inside.

Salvation is a free gift from God, it is simply received through faith in Jesus Christ.

If you would like to receive salvation and begin a relationship with Jesus, then pray this prayer from your heart:

> *I believe in Jesus Christ, the Son of the living God. I believe that He died on a cross for me, and that God has raised Him from the dead and that He is alive. I ask You to come into my heart today, Jesus, and be the Lord of my life, and my best friend. Thank you that You have given me new and eternal life. Thank you that You have made me a brand new creature, and I receive by faith the washing away and forgiveness of every wrong thing I have ever done. Thank you that I am saved.*

Thank you that I am born again, and that from now on You help me to live my new life knowing You more and more, and enjoying the life that you have given me. I ask all this in the name of Jesus. Amen.

Congratulations! You have just made the best decision of your life.

PRAYER FOR THE BAPTISM OF THE HOLY SPIRIT

Jesus said to His disciples,

> *If you then, being evil, know how to give good gifts to your children, how much more will your heavenly Father give the Holy Spirit to those who ask Him!*
>
> ***(Luke 11:13)***

Heavenly Father, I am asking You, in the name of Jesus, that You give me and fill me with Your Holy Spirit, with the

evidence of speaking in other tongues. I believe that when I ask, You give, so thank You that I have received the Holy Spirit right now into my life, in Jesus' mighty name!
Amen.

FAITH ACTION

Believe you have received! Thank God for filling you with the Holy Spirit, and start to praise Him. Speak also with the new words and syllables that you receive. They may sound strange to you at first, but continue to speak. The Holy Spirit will not force you to speak, you have to make the utterance with your mouth, but He will be speaking the heavenly language through you.

ABOUT THE AUTHORS

Billy and Kirsty Lummis serve in Family Church, a multi-congregational church located on the south coast of England. Billy and Kirsty teach discipleship courses, and run a regular Bible study group. Billy also lectures in Faith Works Bible College, Portsmouth.

Billy and Kirsty are passionate about teaching the body of Christ through the truth of the Word of God.

Billy and Kirsty have a young son, Ezra.

billylummis.uk

SERVE

Serve is an imprint of Great Big Life Publishing, a company dedicated to helping authors get their work published. If you have a manuscript that you would like to have considered for publication, please contact us at:

Great Big Life Publishing
Empower Centre
83-87 Kingston Road
Portsmouth
PO2 7DX
info@greatbiglifepublishing.com

Visit our website to see our full catalogue:
greatbiglifepublishing.com